# Welcome Baby!

# Baby Shower Invite

ATTACH BABY SHOWER
INVITATION

♥

♥

# Baby Shower Details

Date

_____

Hosts

_____

Time

_____

Baby Shower Theme

_____

Place

_____

How Many Weeks Pregnant Was Mama?

_____

# Guest

NAME AND RELATIONSHIP TO PARENTS

_____

_____

ADVICE FOR PARENTS

_____

_____

_____

WISHES FOR BABY

_____

_____

_____

# Guest

### NAME AND RELATIONSHIP TO PARENTS

_____

_____

### ADVICE FOR PARENTS

_____

_____

_____

### WISHES FOR BABY

_____

_____

_____

# Guest

## NAME AND RELATIONSHIP TO PARENTS

_____

_____

## ADVICE FOR PARENTS

_____

_____

_____

## WISHES FOR BABY

_____

_____

_____

# Guest

NAME AND RELATIONSHIP TO PARENTS

_____

_____

ADVICE FOR PARENTS

_____

_____

_____

WISHES FOR BABY

_____

_____

_____

# Guest

## NAME AND RELATIONSHIP TO PARENTS

_____

_____

## ADVICE FOR PARENTS

_____

_____

_____

## WISHES FOR BABY

_____

_____

_____

# Guest

NAME AND RELATIONSHIP TO PARENTS

_____

_____

ADVICE FOR PARENTS

_____

_____

_____

WISHES FOR BABY

_____

_____

_____

# Guest

NAME AND RELATIONSHIP TO PARENTS

_____

_____

ADVICE FOR PARENTS

_____

_____

_____

WISHES FOR BABY

_____

_____

_____

# Guest

NAME AND RELATIONSHIP TO PARENTS

_____

_____

ADVICE FOR PARENTS

_____

_____

_____

WISHES FOR BABY

_____

_____

_____

# Guest

NAME AND RELATIONSHIP TO PARENTS

_____

_____

ADVICE FOR PARENTS

_____

_____

_____

WISHES FOR BABY

_____

_____

_____

# Guest

NAME AND RELATIONSHIP TO PARENTS

_____

_____

ADVICE FOR PARENTS

_____

_____

_____

WISHES FOR BABY

_____

_____

_____

# Guest

NAME AND RELATIONSHIP TO PARENTS

_____

_____

ADVICE FOR PARENTS

_____

_____

_____

WISHES FOR BABY

_____

_____

_____

# Guest

NAME AND RELATIONSHIP TO PARENTS

_____

_____

ADVICE FOR PARENTS

_____

_____

_____

WISHES FOR BABY

_____

_____

_____

# Guest

### NAME AND RELATIONSHIP TO PARENTS

_____

_____

### ADVICE FOR PARENTS

_____

_____

_____

### WISHES FOR BABY

_____

_____

_____

# Guest

NAME AND RELATIONSHIP TO PARENTS

_____

_____

ADVICE FOR PARENTS

_____

_____

_____

WISHES FOR BABY

_____

_____

_____

# Guest

## NAME AND RELATIONSHIP TO PARENTS

_____

_____

## ADVICE FOR PARENTS

_____

_____

_____

## WISHES FOR BABY

_____

_____

_____

# Guest

## NAME AND RELATIONSHIP TO PARENTS

_____

_____

## ADVICE FOR PARENTS

_____

_____

_____

## WISHES FOR BABY

_____

_____

_____

# Guest

NAME AND RELATIONSHIP TO PARENTS

_____

_____

ADVICE FOR PARENTS

_____

_____

_____

WISHES FOR BABY

_____

_____

_____

## Guest

NAME AND RELATIONSHIP TO PARENTS

_____

_____

ADVICE FOR PARENTS

_____

_____

_____

WISHES FOR BABY

_____

_____

_____

# Guest

## NAME AND RELATIONSHIP TO PARENTS

_____

_____

## ADVICE FOR PARENTS

_____

_____

_____

## WISHES FOR BABY

_____

_____

_____

# Guest

## NAME AND RELATIONSHIP TO PARENTS

_____

_____

## ADVICE FOR PARENTS

_____

_____

_____

## WISHES FOR BABY

_____

_____

_____

# Guest

## NAME AND RELATIONSHIP TO PARENTS

_____

_____

## ADVICE FOR PARENTS

_____

_____

_____

## WISHES FOR BABY

_____

_____

_____

# Guest

NAME AND RELATIONSHIP TO PARENTS

_____

_____

ADVICE FOR PARENTS

_____

_____

_____

WISHES FOR BABY

_____

_____

_____

# Guest

NAME AND RELATIONSHIP TO PARENTS

_____

_____

ADVICE FOR PARENTS

_____

_____

_____

WISHES FOR BABY

_____

_____

_____

# Guest

NAME AND RELATIONSHIP TO PARENTS

_____

_____

ADVICE FOR PARENTS

_____

_____

_____

WISHES FOR BABY

_____

_____

_____

# Guest

### NAME AND RELATIONSHIP TO PARENTS

_____

_____

### ADVICE FOR PARENTS

_____

_____

_____

### WISHES FOR BABY

_____

_____

_____

# Guest

NAME AND RELATIONSHIP TO PARENTS

_____

_____

ADVICE FOR PARENTS

_____

_____

_____

WISHES FOR BABY

_____

_____

_____

# Guest

## NAME AND RELATIONSHIP TO PARENTS

_____

_____

## ADVICE FOR PARENTS

_____

_____

_____

## WISHES FOR BABY

_____

_____

_____

# Guest

## NAME AND RELATIONSHIP TO PARENTS

_____

_____

## ADVICE FOR PARENTS

_____

_____

## WISHES FOR BABY

_____

_____

_____

# Guest

NAME AND RELATIONSHIP TO PARENTS

_____

_____

ADVICE FOR PARENTS

_____

_____

_____

WISHES FOR BABY

_____

_____

_____

# Guest

NAME AND RELATIONSHIP TO PARENTS

_____

_____

ADVICE FOR PARENTS

_____

_____

_____

WISHES FOR BABY

_____

_____

_____

# Guest

## NAME AND RELATIONSHIP TO PARENTS

_____

_____

## ADVICE FOR PARENTS

_____

_____

_____

## WISHES FOR BABY

_____

_____

_____

# Guest

## NAME AND RELATIONSHIP TO PARENTS

_____

_____

## ADVICE FOR PARENTS

_____

_____

_____

## WISHES FOR BABY

_____

_____

_____

# Guest

## NAME AND RELATIONSHIP TO PARENTS

## ADVICE FOR PARENTS

## WISHES FOR BABY

# Guest

NAME AND RELATIONSHIP TO PARENTS

_____

_____

ADVICE FOR PARENTS

_____

_____

_____

WISHES FOR BABY

_____

_____

_____

## NAME AND RELATIONSHIP TO PARENTS

_____

_____

## ADVICE FOR PARENTS

_____

_____

_____

## WISHES FOR BABY

_____

_____

_____

# Guest

NAME AND RELATIONSHIP TO PARENTS

_____

_____

ADVICE FOR PARENTS

_____

_____

_____

WISHES FOR BABY

_____

_____

_____

# Guest

## NAME AND RELATIONSHIP TO PARENTS

_____

_____

## ADVICE FOR PARENTS

_____

_____

_____

## WISHES FOR BABY

_____

_____

_____

# Guest

## NAME AND RELATIONSHIP TO PARENTS

_____

_____

## ADVICE FOR PARENTS

_____

_____

_____

## WISHES FOR BABY

_____

_____

_____

# Guest

### NAME AND RELATIONSHIP TO PARENTS

_____

_____

### ADVICE FOR PARENTS

_____

_____

_____

### WISHES FOR BABY

_____

_____

_____

# Guest

NAME AND RELATIONSHIP TO PARENTS

_____

_____

ADVICE FOR PARENTS

_____

_____

_____

WISHES FOR BABY

_____

_____

_____

# Guest

## NAME AND RELATIONSHIP TO PARENTS

_____

_____

## ADVICE FOR PARENTS

_____

_____

_____

## WISHES FOR BABY

_____

_____

_____

# Guest

## NAME AND RELATIONSHIP TO PARENTS

_____

_____

## ADVICE FOR PARENTS

_____

_____

_____

## WISHES FOR BABY

_____

_____

_____

# Guest

## NAME AND RELATIONSHIP TO PARENTS

_____

_____

## ADVICE FOR PARENTS

_____

_____

_____

## WISHES FOR BABY

_____

_____

_____

# Guest

NAME AND RELATIONSHIP TO PARENTS

_____

_____

ADVICE FOR PARENTS

_____

_____

_____

WISHES FOR BABY

_____

_____

_____

# Guest

## NAME AND RELATIONSHIP TO PARENTS

_____

_____

## ADVICE FOR PARENTS

_____

_____

_____

## WISHES FOR BABY

_____

_____

_____

# Guest

NAME AND RELATIONSHIP TO PARENTS

_____

_____

ADVICE FOR PARENTS

_____

_____

_____

WISHES FOR BABY

_____

_____

_____

# Guest

### NAME AND RELATIONSHIP TO PARENTS

_____

_____

### ADVICE FOR PARENTS

_____

_____

_____

### WISHES FOR BABY

_____

_____

_____

# Guest

NAME AND RELATIONSHIP TO PARENTS

_____

_____

ADVICE FOR PARENTS

_____

_____

_____

WISHES FOR BABY

_____

_____

_____

# Guest

### NAME AND RELATIONSHIP TO PARENTS

_____

_____

### ADVICE FOR PARENTS

_____

_____

_____

### WISHES FOR BABY

_____

_____

_____

# Guest

NAME AND RELATIONSHIP TO PARENTS

_____

_____

ADVICE FOR PARENTS

_____

_____

_____

WISHES FOR BABY

_____

_____

_____

# Guest

NAME AND RELATIONSHIP TO PARENTS

_____

_____

ADVICE FOR PARENTS

_____

_____

_____

WISHES FOR BABY

_____

_____

_____

# Guest

NAME AND RELATIONSHIP TO PARENTS

_____

_____

ADVICE FOR PARENTS

_____

_____

_____

WISHES FOR BABY

_____

_____

_____

# Guest

## NAME AND RELATIONSHIP TO PARENTS

_____

_____

## ADVICE FOR PARENTS

_____

_____

_____

## WISHES FOR BABY

_____

_____

_____

# Guest

NAME AND RELATIONSHIP TO PARENTS

_____

_____

ADVICE FOR PARENTS

_____

_____

_____

WISHES FOR BABY

_____

_____

_____

# Guest

NAME AND RELATIONSHIP TO PARENTS

_____

_____

ADVICE FOR PARENTS

_____

_____

_____

WISHES FOR BABY

_____

_____

_____

## Guest

NAME AND RELATIONSHIP TO PARENTS

_____

_____

ADVICE FOR PARENTS

_____

_____

_____

WISHES FOR BABY

_____

_____

_____

# Guest

## NAME AND RELATIONSHIP TO PARENTS

_____

_____

## ADVICE FOR PARENTS

_____

_____

_____

## WISHES FOR BABY

_____

_____

_____

# Guest

NAME AND RELATIONSHIP TO PARENTS

_____

_____

ADVICE FOR PARENTS

_____

_____

_____

WISHES FOR BABY

_____

_____

_____

# Guest

NAME AND RELATIONSHIP TO PARENTS

_____

_____

ADVICE FOR PARENTS

_____

_____

_____

WISHES FOR BABY

_____

_____

_____

# Guest

NAME AND RELATIONSHIP TO PARENTS

_____

_____

ADVICE FOR PARENTS

_____

_____

_____

WISHES FOR BABY

_____

_____

_____

# Guest

## NAME AND RELATIONSHIP TO PARENTS

_____

_____

## ADVICE FOR PARENTS

_____

_____

_____

## WISHES FOR BABY

_____

_____

_____

# Guest

NAME AND RELATIONSHIP TO PARENTS

_____

_____

ADVICE FOR PARENTS

_____

_____

_____

WISHES FOR BABY

_____

_____

_____

# Guest

## NAME AND RELATIONSHIP TO PARENTS

_____

_____

## ADVICE FOR PARENTS

_____

_____

_____

## WISHES FOR BABY

_____

_____

_____

# Guest

### NAME AND RELATIONSHIP TO PARENTS

_____

_____

### ADVICE FOR PARENTS

_____

_____

_____

### WISHES FOR BABY

_____

_____

_____

# Guest

NAME AND RELATIONSHIP TO PARENTS

_____

_____

ADVICE FOR PARENTS

_____

_____

_____

WISHES FOR BABY

_____

_____

_____

# Guest

## NAME AND RELATIONSHIP TO PARENTS

_____

_____

## ADVICE FOR PARENTS

_____

_____

_____

## WISHES FOR BABY

_____

_____

_____

# Guest

## NAME AND RELATIONSHIP TO PARENTS

_____

_____

## ADVICE FOR PARENTS

_____

_____

_____

## WISHES FOR BABY

_____

_____

_____

# Guest

NAME AND RELATIONSHIP TO PARENTS

_____

_____

ADVICE FOR PARENTS

_____

_____

_____

WISHES FOR BABY

_____

_____

_____

# Guest

## NAME AND RELATIONSHIP TO PARENTS

_____

_____

## ADVICE FOR PARENTS

_____

_____

_____

## WISHES FOR BABY

_____

_____

_____

# Guest

## NAME AND RELATIONSHIP TO PARENTS

_____

_____

## ADVICE FOR PARENTS

_____

_____

_____

## WISHES FOR BABY

_____

_____

_____

# Guest

## NAME AND RELATIONSHIP TO PARENTS

_____

_____

## ADVICE FOR PARENTS

_____

_____

_____

## WISHES FOR BABY

_____

_____

_____

# Guest

NAME AND RELATIONSHIP TO PARENTS

_____

_____

ADVICE FOR PARENTS

_____

_____

_____

WISHES FOR BABY

_____

_____

_____

# Guest

## NAME AND RELATIONSHIP TO PARENTS

_____

_____

## ADVICE FOR PARENTS

_____

_____

_____

## WISHES FOR BABY

_____

_____

_____

## Games We Played

_____

_____

_____

## Food we ate

_____

_____

_____

## Music Played

_____

_____

_____

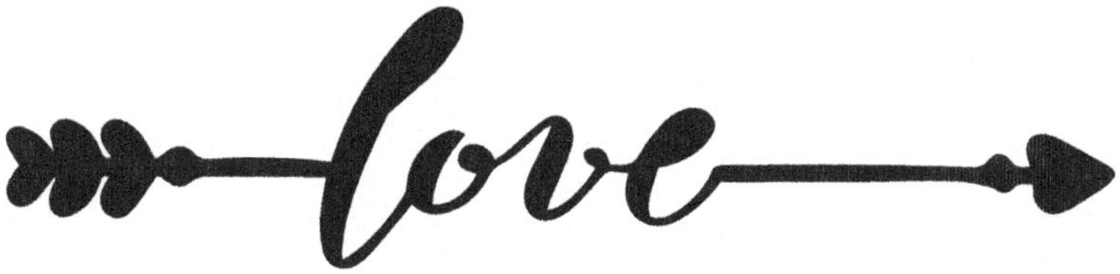
love

attach keepsakes & pictures

attach keepsakes & pictures

attach keepsakes & pictures

attach keepsakes & pictures

# GIFT LOG

# 🎁 GIFT LOG

| GIFT RECEIVED | GIVEN BY |
|---|---|
| | |
| | |
| | |
| | |
| | |
| | |
| | |
| | |
| | |

 # GIFT LOG

| GIFT RECEIVED | GIVEN BY |
|---|---|
| | |
| | |
| | |
| | |
| | |
| | |
| | |
| | |

# 🎁 GIFT LOG

| GIFT RECEIVED | GIVEN BY |
|---|---|
| | |
| | |
| | |
| | |
| | |
| | |
| | |
| | |
| | |

# 🎁 GIFT LOG

| GIFT RECEIVED | GIVEN BY |
|---|---|
| | |
| | |
| | |
| | |
| | |
| | |
| | |
| | |
| | |

# 🎁 GIFT LOG

| GIFT RECEIVED | GIVEN BY |
|---|---|
| | |
| | |
| | |
| | |
| | |
| | |
| | |
| | |
| | |

 # GIFT LOG

| GIFT RECEIVED | GIVEN BY |
|---|---|
| | |
| | |
| | |
| | |
| | |
| | |
| | |
| | |
| | |
| | |

# 🎁 GIFT LOG

| GIFT RECEIVED | GIVEN BY |
|---|---|
| | |
| | |
| | |
| | |
| | |
| | |
| | |
| | |
| | |

# 🎁 GIFT LOG

| GIFT RECEIVED | GIVEN BY |
|---|---|
| | |
| | |
| | |
| | |
| | |
| | |
| | |
| | |
| | |

# 🎁 GIFT LOG

| GIFT RECEIVED | GIVEN BY |
|---|---|
| | |
| | |
| | |
| | |
| | |
| | |
| | |
| | |
| | |

Made in the USA
Monee, IL
21 June 2023

36464371R00063